The U Journey
Jesus at the centre

By Michelle Mapplebeck

This is my story, about the unexpected paths through this journey called life and the different seasons we may face. This is one that touched me mightily but how my walk with the Lord Jesus, helped me and walked me through.

I hope you enjoy reading this book and it encourages you with your own walk with Jesus.

If you don't know this Jesus, I am talking about, I hope it inspires you to find and seek Him for yourself.

As I was writing, this verse came to mind: -

Hebrews 12 1-2

Therefore, since we are surrounded by such a great cloud of witnesses, let us throw off everything that hinders and sin that so easily entangles. And let us run with perseverance the race marked before us, fixing our eyes on Jesus, the pioneer and perfecter of faith. For the joy set before Him, He endured the cross, scorning its shame and sat down at the right hand of the throne of God.
(NIV)

Contents

Chapter 1
The Path of Life   4

Chapter 2
The Beginning   6

Chapter 3
The Unexpected Journey
A Different Kind of Chapter   9

Chapter 4
The Unbeaten Track   18

Chapter 5
Jesus At the Centre   25

Chapter 6
A Different Kind of Message   31

The right of Michelle Mapplebeck to be identified as the author of this work has been asserted in accordance with the Copyright, Designs and Patents Act 1988. All rights reserved.

ISBN: 978-1-910779-02-6

No part of this publication may be reproduced, stored in a retrieval system, or transmitted, in any form or by any means, electronic, mechanical, photocopying, recording or otherwise, without the prior permission of the copyright owners

First Published by Michelle Mapplebeck 2023
Typeset by Oxford eBooks.

Chapter 1
The Path of Life

I want to start this chapter with a bible verse.

Isaiah 41–10
Fear not, for I am with you, Be not dismayed, for I am your God.
I will strengthen you, Yes, I will help you.
I will uphold you with My righteous right hand.

This is a promise the Lord God of heaven and earth said, He will Never leave us or forsake us.

So, no matter what you are facing, God is with you, even if we don't feel him.

There is a poem call footstep in the sand, if you have never read it, I encourage you to do.

It's such a picture of God's love through His son Jesus and how we are never alone.

1 Peter 5–6
Cast ALL your cares on Him Because He cares for You.

If you have had hard times or even walking through the valley, as you are reading this and have been asking yourself, where God is in all of this. He is right beside you. As you read the pages of this book you will see how in my journey, this is true.

Psalm 23 v 1–6

The Lord is My Shepherd,
I shall not want.
He makes me to lie down in green pastures,
He leads me beside the still waters.
He restores my soul,
He leads me in the paths of righteousness.
For His name's sake.
Yea, though I walk through the valley of the shadow of death,
I will fear no evil,
For You are with me,
Your rod and Your staff, the comfort me.
You prepare a table for me in the presence of my enemies,
You anoint my head with oil,
My cup runs over.
Surely goodness and mercy shall follow me all the days of my life,
And I will dwell in the house of the Lord.
Forever and ever.

Chapter 2
The Beginning

So, I am Michelle, my husband's name is Kevin and we have been married now for nearly 7 years. We got married on 16th April 2016.

What an amazing day that was, I married my best friend. God brought us together and what a journey we have had. We have been, to some amazing places.

One of my favourites, being Israel, the year after we got married. We got to walk the roads and paths that Jesus did. What an experience.

Me and Kev were both Christians when we got married, meaning we are followers of Jesus Christ. We believe in the bible, we believe Jesus was born of a virgin, fully man and God.

We believe in Jesus's death and resurrection from the dead. This was to give us the gift of new life in Him, when we accept Jesus into our hearts and ask Him to be our Lord and saviour.

If you have never read about this Jesus, I am talking about, get at bible NIV, NKJV and read Matthew, Mark, Luke and John.

Before me and Kev got married, I asked the Lord if this was the man for me? I believe he was, so I asked the Lord to confirm this. I had heard that Christians have to ask the Lord a specific question. So, I asked if this is the man, Lord? He will propose on the west wood up near Hull. It was a very special place for me, we would go for nice walk up there and I really enjoyed going. When Kev proposed, he did ask me on the west wood. I said yes. Like I said we are just coming up to our 7th year wedding anniversary.

Me and Kev always wanted a family, we would talk about it and pick out names we liked. We would mess about and say to the kids, "get down" or "stop doing this or that." We believed that someday we would have children, all in the Lord's timing.

So, you can imagine our joy, when the day came. We took a pregnancy test and it was positive, Saturday 16th January 2021. All our hopes and dreams made real; we were so happy.

I can't even explain, just how excited we were. We told our families and close friend. We thanked God for answering our prayers. We told everyone, as we were so ecstatic. We were roughly about two months, maybe a bit more. What an amazing gift. We were so excited, we dreamed of what the future holds and how life would change.

I told the ladies at work. We told everyone. How exciting, this was actually happening. We had been waiting, four and a half years for this news. We were going to be parents. A precious gift from above.

Psalm 139 v 13–16

For you formed my inward parts; You covered me in my mother's womb.

I praise You, for I am fearfully and wonderfully made.

Marvelous are Your works, And that my soul knows very well.

My frame was not hidden from You, When I was made in secret,

And skilfully wrought in the lowest part of the earth.

Your eyes saw my substance, being yet unformed.

And in Your book, they were all written, the days fashioned for me,

When as yet there were none of them.

Chapter 3
The Unexpected Journey
A Different Kind of Chapter

So, like I said Saturday 16st of January, was one of the best days of our lives and we were so excited. We told everyone. I felt the Lord give me pictures of how our baby looked. I would search, for pictures on the internet to show Kev. We were so excited; this was actually happening. Our baby was coming. A new chapter for us.

My body was changing, I felt different. This was really happening, it started to feel real. I knew our baby was down in the depth of my womb being formed. I believe we were having a girl. We chose her name, Chloe Louise Mapplebeck. What a blessing this baby would be.

We went to buy a boy's outfit just in case! I was starting to feel uncomfortable in my normal clothes and was looking at getting some maternity stuff. Excitement, as well as an uncertainty of what the future would hold. This was our first pregnancy.

The unknown was in front of us but we would embrace it, with both hands. The Lord is with us and we have each other. I rang the doctors to book an appointment with the midwife.

A week later, on the Sunday, I felt really funny and later on I started to spot bleed. I rang my friend, who used to be a midwife, she said that this can be normal, if it was an implantation bleed, but that if it gets worse to ring the doctors. So, I had an early night, the pain got worse around 11, then I woke early hours of the morning bleeding heavily and in tremendous amount of pain. I rang the NHS line, they advised me to go to hospital. The nearest hospital was Walsgrave Coventry, the weather was so bad, mixture of snow and ice. I said to Kev I can't sit in the car, so I rang for an ambulance.

Even now I look back and I can see God's hand over everything. A lady and a man came, they were so nice and kind to me. The lady checked me over, the man stayed quiet on the other side of the room. It was during the time we had lockdown.

She said I was fine, but she thought I was having a miscarriage. She told me to get as comfortable as I could and take another pregnancy test in a few days. She said that she had miscarried with her first baby too, but had gone on to have a healthy pregnancy. She was so kind to me.

The next morning felt like a blur, I remember getting up in the morning and asking Kev, if last night was real. It felt like a dream, he held me and we cried. He had no words; I could see the emotion in his face. A whirlwind of emotions.

I couldn't make any sense of what was happening, just a blur. We took another pregnancy test on the Wednesday, still pregnant. I believed she was still in there. I rang the doctors and they gave me the number for Walsgrave early pregnancy unit. I rang them and got an urgent appointment, in the afternoon. Kev wasn't allowed in as it was in the covid pandemic. I sat in the waiting room on my own, I could see Kev waiting outside the doors for me. They called me in, they checked me over gave me an internal scan. She didn't really say anything, or I can't remember if she did, she took blood tests. I can't really remember what happened, it was a blur.

I felt numb, it was like being in a dream and at any minute we would wake up and all would be fine. The Thursday night the pain was unbearable, we went to Walsgrave again, another trip to the hospital. This time Kev came in with me, this was a journey we were taking together, not just me. Even though the journey through loss is different for men and women, it's still as heart-breaking and painful for both. It's still the loss of their child, still an aching for what should of and could have been. Loss is such a hard journey. I remember asking the Lord and crying out to Him, Why Lord, why us?

Also, in the middle of the pain and loss, you will probably know someone who has just found out they are pregnant or who is pregnant. This makes this so much more raw and hurtful, more question, why them and not me. Grief in its rawist form, there are many different stages to grief. Shock, Denial, Anger and Guilt, Despair and Depression, Acceptance.

You may have some of these or you may feel all of them. I think at first, I was still in shock. The Thursday night again I felt the Lord's hand over this and as I look back, I know it was.

I am going to stop here for a moment, I feel some of you may ask, where was your God in this? Or even, why did He let this happen? My answer: - bad and good happen to everyone, no one is exempted. We live in a fallen world, look back in the book of Genesis, in the bible God created everything perfect and then man sinned against God. Sin means going our own way and doing things our own way, not the way God ordained it. Jesus came to be the perfect sacrifice the way back to God the Father.

Romans 3 v 22–24

> *Even the righteousness of God through faith in Jesus Christ, to all and on all who believe. For there is no difference; for All have sinned and fallen short of the Glory of God, being justified freely by His grace through the redemption that is Jesus Christ.*

Jesus Christ and His sacrifice on the cross redeem us from our sin and gives us the pathway back to God. If we believe in Him and Trust in His name.

Thursday night, there were a few couples in

front of us, a longish wait. I was praying for a lady as she sobbed hysterically in the doorway with her partner. Then our turn, I asked for Kev to come in, the doctor took us to the examination room but someone was in there. So, she took us to a quiet room, I believe this was God. As I look back, I see my God hand over everything.

My eyes are filling with tears as I re-live this time. She sat us down and I asked what was happening? Was our baby gone? She was so kind to us, softly spoken words. I keep looking at Kev to try and make out what was going on. To make sense of what was happening. I couldn't the fog, the numbness, the bewilderment. I couldn't think straight. I looked to Kev for comfort, I couldn't understand. What was happening? my baby? Our baby?

I don't remember everything; I was still in shock and numb for the pain and the whirlwind of the last few days. I believe we both were. It was like living in a dream but more a nightmare, waiting to wake up any minute. But it didn't happen, this was real. I don't remember all she said but she said she was sorry and that she knew this baby was wanted. How could she know that from sitting with us 5 minutes?

She was of course so right! Our baby was so wanted. She examined me again and sent me home with strong pain relief. We had another appointment on the Friday, for more blood test. The next few weeks were in and out of

Walsgrave for appointments. The hospital staff were great, I couldn't fault them.

I had time off work; we also made an appointment to see out pastor at church. The first one I believe; I was still in shock and the realisation had not yet hit me. We had gone from the hospital straight to church. I was just going through the motions at first, as this is what people do when things are bad, but I never expected this would be such a significant part of this journey.

We had regular meetings with our pastor and he was an amazing support. The whirl wind carried on. Some days were such a struggle, just to get up and start the day. Just to get out of bed and get dressed. If this is you well done, small steps, one thing at a time, is a massive achievement. Be kind to yourself. Many of my morning prayers were Lord help me through the day, I can't do this without you.

I went back to work, only some of the ladies knew why I was off, so I had to tell everyone that our baby had gone. The pain and the reality of this truth cut like a knife. How life had changed in a few weeks, it was devastating. Still trying to make sense of it all, still asking why? Still wondering. Our world crashing around us as we stood helplessly and watched.

I worked in a nursery, not the best place to be when you have just lost your baby. I was in the toddler room, the age where mums most often fell pregnant again. Blow after blow, parents coming in announcing their pregnancy. Day after day watching mums with growing baby bumps. So hard it was like someone was stabbing me each time.

I went in day after day. I would smile, I would do my job but the point came when reality hit and hit hard the final blow. Enough was enough. I knew my baby had gone, the life I had felt and that had stared to change me inside had now gone. I craved for what was there but now empty. I was walking through the valley, I was in the dark, gloomy place but it got worse, reality hit and knocked me off my feet. I still couldn't believe this had happened, but now I couldn't function. Day after day of carrying this pain, this deep-down ache inside me. Watching pregnant women, babies and children all day long broke me. If you knew me, I am not like that at all. I am a happy individual, take life as it comes but this absolutely and total floored me. The day came that I broke, I cried at work, I broke down.

No more just getting on with it, no more. I could not take anymore. It was like I had a mirror and people could see the mirror. All was fine in the mirror but underneath it was like the bottom had fallen out. I kept going, kept pushing myself, things would be ok, just keep going. The day came that I literally fell apart, no more keeping going, no more pushing, no more.

I had finally broken, day after day of pushing myself, had finally taken its toll and I broke. The tears came, I couldn't stop them, I couldn't function. I could not deal with everyday life. I had lost our baby and I was broken. I had no idea how or where to start.

We went to see our pastor; he was so good. I explained how I was feeling. When you can't make head or tail of anything, it's good to have someone on the outside to come alongside you. He drew us a diagram of a river flowing, then he drew a big drop, at the bottom of the drop he said, "this is where the water crashed together, turning this way and that". He said, "you have been going along the river nicely but then you have had this massive drop/fall just like a waterfall". Then he pointed to the bottom and said, "you are here". Right down at the bottom of the waterfall. He was right, that is exactly where I was and how I felt. Not knowing if I was coming or going. Not even being able to make sense of anything, let alone function. It was reassuring to know that this is a normal response to such a traumatic incident. I felt in the darkness and unable to function. It we think of a waterfall for a minute, the noise as it hits the bottom. The water is so churned up, the force of the water from the fall as it hits the bottom, the impact at the bottom. This was a normal reaction to what had happened. Again,

let's just look at the different stages of grief:
- Shock, Denial, Anger and Guilt, Despair and Depression, Acceptance. I was in despair.

Chapter 4
The Unbeaten Track

Before I go on, I want to share something with you, I wrote a diary over the first few months of this journey. It pains me to read it, but I want to share this with you.

I held a boy in my arms at nursery yesterday and he feel asleep...

I felt the Lord say this to me after -
"That's how I hold you,
You may not feel Me, But I have you,
holding You close at all times."

I thanked the Lord for such a word, I felt so lost going through this. This comforted me. My friend said to me, "In a storm when the pilot can't see, He has to fly by instruments only." I believe this was that time for me, but God in His mercy gave me these wonderful and comforting words.

My journal bible verse for that day was this-

Matthew 11 v 28
Come to me, all you who labour and are heavy laden and I will give you rest.

What a promise, God is so good to us. No matter what we are going through He is there close then close even when we don't feel Him.

We had regular meetings at church, after a while Kev started to open up too. This was a blessing for both of us.

I got a book from our church that a lady had written called: -

Little Fingers Never Alone in The Shadows – A gift for the bereaved parent
by Charlotte Nail
https://www.littlefingers.org.uk

This really helped me, I read it daily. Some days, I could identify with the feeling on the pages. It encouraged me, it was about a caterpillar turning into a butterfly. This book was so helpful. It had lots of useful information and contact details. One of the contacts was the miscarriage association. I rang them for support on a number of occasions.

The Lord was so good to me, He started to draw me to people at church that had been through the same thing. A guy at our church was speaking one Sunday, he shared he had 3 heavenly children. I spoke to him after, I just cried. Tears are also part of the healing process. I had bottled these feeling up for so long, that now if I cried, I couldn't stop. So, I just let them flow. We are fearfully and wonderfully made, God has made us so incredible, that when we have strong emotions, we cry. Jesus, when He walked this earth also had the same emotion we do.

Hebrews 4 v 15-16

For we do not have a High Priest (Jesus) who cannot sympathize with our weakness, but was in all points tempted as we are, yet without sin. Let us therefore come boldly to the throne of grace, that we may obtain mercy and find grace to help in times of need.

My diary date March 16th 2021,

So today two months ago we found out we were pregnant. What a rollercoaster ride it has been. Lord, I thank you that you showed me the picture of you holding me, like that boy I was holding. Lord, we celebrate today with thanks giving, prayers, tears, sadness, happiness. It's a mixed bag.

A song *Goodness of God* came to mind: -
  I love you Lord,
  for your mercy never fail me,
  In darkest night you are there like no other.
  I know you as a Father,
  I know you as a friend and I have lived in the goodness of God.

Lord, I give you this day and no matter what it holds. I give it to you. Help me, lead and guide me and strengthen me.

Romans 5 v 5
Now hope does not disappoint because the love of God has been poured out in our hearts by the Holy Spirit who was given us.

Romans 15 v 13
Now may the God of Hope fill you with all joy and peace in believing that you may abound in Hope by the power of the Holy Spirit.

The Lord was speaking through His word to me, at this most difficult time reassuring me that He was with me and the power of Gods Holy Spirit was with me and He would give me hope, strength and peace.

Again, this has been a healing journey, now not only over months but also now years. God is faithful to us because of His love for us. I still have days, to this day where something will be a trigger to me and hit me as hard as it did then. There have been some days, which still are such a hard journey to walk along. I remember being on a call with the miscarriage association, on zoom due to lockdown and not being able to meet. A lady was on there and it had been 6 months from her miscarriage and she was so broken. The tears just flowed, it was heart breaking to hear and witness. Foolishly, I thought, "I hope I am still not like that after that time" but of course I was! You have triggers throughout a pregnancy or mile- stones at different stages. Triggers can be a person, place, thing or situation that brings about an intense or unexpected emotional response. These can happen any time and anywhere and it is totally normal, the emotion can be very over whelming.

Be kind to yourself, you will have good days and bad days. If you need to cry. then cry. If you need to sleep, then sleep, go for a walk, do a little shopping. Have a bath, go for a massage, do things that you enjoy. Do something you enjoy daily, read a book, make that time for you. Be kind to yourself. Its very, very important, and one of the hardest things to do.

It was a big lesson for me to learn, just to do that but I had to learn to take time out and do things for me. I enjoyed a bath with relaxing music with birds and snow. The Lord was very close to me. It was very hard as it was lock down and we could not go out anywhere and we could not see our families. This made this journey so much harder; we probably would have had day trips out and seen our friend and family. Eventually things did start to open up and we did have days out and visited friends and family. We also got to go back to church when it opened back up, I think it was May time. That was such a blessing for us.

I remember one day we went out. I wasn't having the best day, I felt very vulnerable, emotions were running high. We went out to a house and gardens for the day. There behind us, was a heavily pregnant lady following us around. It was like another punch in the face. A trigger if you will, I just wanted her to leave. We hurried on and left them behind. It's like when you buy a new car you never see it (or you don't pay attention to it) but when you have that car you see it everywhere. It's the same here. It's like having an open wound and someone coming up with a bag of salt, here have this... It's so hard. I get it.

I will say through this mess, God really brought us closer together in our marriage. We learned to talk to each other and express our feelings, spending time listening to the other. This can be very hard for couples to do but God really helped us open up to each other and share our feelings. When something like this happens, it can be easy to bury our feeling and not talk about them but this can lead to other problems which surface in other ways; like unresolved anger, resentment, feeling neglected or the other doesn't care. This can cause a wedge in your marriage.

Romans 5 v 1–5

Therefore, having been justified by faith, we have peace with God through our Lord Jesus Christ, through whom also we have access by faith into the grace in which we stand, and rejoice in the hope of the glory of God. And not only that, but we also glory in tribulations, knowing that tribulations produces perseverance and perseverance, character and character hope. Now hope does not disappointed, because the love of God has been poured out in our hearts by the Holy Spirit who was given to us.

Chapter 5
Jesus At the Centre

Psalm 91 v 2

I will say of the Lord.
"He is my refuge and my fortress,
My God, in Him I will Trust."

I had to hold on in the hard times, God has always walked with me through my life and He was not about to leave me now. I held on tight, I prayed, I read my bible. Jesus led me through and held my hand.

This is how intimate my God is, my Emmanuel God with me.

On the March 17th 2021, me and Kev went down to the canal to lay some flowers for our baby girl and to say goodbye. This was still lock down, I had been praying on the way that God would get someone to pray for us. It was a very difficult day for us and I wanted God's comfort. We walked by the canal and then up by the church. The doors were open, so I went in, on the floor was the cross of Jesus and the word underneath Hope and Dream.

The church leader came over and started to talk to us, I shared with her and she prayed for us. I thank the Lord for this answer to prayer and His encouragement. I kept a diary when I was going through this hard time. God is speaking all the time but are we listening?

March 25th 2021, I read the book The Boy, The Mole, The Fox and The Horse, this book encouraged me. The boy falls off the horse in the story, the horse says to the boy

"You Fell but I Got You".

I felt the lord say this to me, "Michelle you fell but I got you". Don't fear or be afraid, I got you. I got this. I am with you; I never leave you.

Lord we fell but you have us, you hold us, you are with us and that is the difference. Again there will be good and bad days but you have and hold us.

I still don't understand all this but.

Isiah 55 v 8

"For My thoughts are not your thoughts, nor are your ways My ways," says the Lord.
"For as the heavens are higher than the earth, so are My ways higher than your ways,
And My thoughts than your thoughts."

April 3rd 2021 – So today I found out, a friend of a friend, is having a baby and yes, it's a girl and yes, the baby will be due around the same time as our baby. I feel someone has pulled the rug from under me, I am getting battered. I can't take any more. The tears won't stop. I am so angry. Lord, I don't understand help me with this pain and emotions.

Psalm 34 v 18
The Lord is close to the brokenhearted: He rescues those whose spirits are crushed.

Unless you have been through this you will never ever know how it feels. I felt someone had grabbed my insides and pulled them out. I fix my eyes on you Jesus, help me through this storm, be my anchor, I cling to you. The tears keep coming, I have learned to just let them come. My hope is lost and my faith is low. I don't understand and I probably never will but I Will Trust You and keep holding on. Lord, I pray you help me in these tough days and keep me close to you.

Psalm 91 v 1–2
He who dwells in the secret place of the Most High. Shall abide under the shadow of the Almighty. I will say of the Lord "He is my refuge and My fortress. My God in Him I will Trust".

The Lord is close to the broken hearted and as we look at Jesus life, we see a close and intimate relationship with God the Father. Jesus too struggled and battled with His feelings. If we look in the gospels, **Matthew 26 v 36** onwards and **Luke 22 v 39** onwards. We see Jesus struggling as His time on earth comes to an end and it's time for Him to endure the Cross. Love poured out for you and me. Jesus was mocked, beaten, spat on, tortured and crucified. Perfect love poured out for us. Jesus struggled, He wrestled, He pleaded and asked God His Father to take this cup of suffering and unbearable pain from Him. The answer was will you do it, Jesus did not need to do it. He did it for us, so we could have a perfect relationship with God the Father, through the Blood of Jesus, that was poured out on the cross. My suffering and pain were a little percentage of what Jesus, my Lord and Savour went through for me.

Matthew 26 v 39

> *Jesus went a little farther and fell on His face, and prayed, saying, "O My Father, if it's possible, let this cup pass from Me; nevertheless, not as I will but as Your will".*

God could see the bigger picture and knew the end of the story. Jesus still had to be willing, obedient to the Father's will. It said Jesus sweated great drops of blood in His anguish. This was not an easy time for Jesus, He knew what was coming and what He would have to endure. Again, Gods ways are not our ways, His thoughts are not our thoughts. God sees the bigger picture.

I encourage you to read The Weaver poem by B.M Franklin.

Matthew 16 v 24
If anyone desires to follow Me, let him deny himself, and take up his cross and follow Me.

We are all going to have troubles in this life but the choice is, do we run to God and ask Him to help and to guide us or do we run from Him and turn our back on Him.

I found this time for us very, very hard, as it was lockdown and everything was closed down, we could not go out, or meet friends. We couldn't talk to friends and family as we did not see them, we couldn't go out because everywhere was closed. It was so hard. I felt the Lord put on my heart to read the book of Job in the Bible. Job is a very heart felt and tragic story, but Job keeps his faith strong. Even when his friends argued with him. They said it had happened because of something Job did, instead of just life circumstances. What a man of faith. God knew we would struggle in this life, so He gave us the Bible to encourage, to speak to us. A living book the very word of God spoken for us. What a privilege and a bless that God so cares for us.

April 10th 2021
We have named our baby Chloe. The Lord has really ministered to me the last few days. God gave me a picture of Him holding our baby Chloe. I could see arm

and in the arms was a baby wrapped up. I know she's safe in your mighty hands Lord.

April 19th 2021

Jesus ministered these lovely words to me in a poem.

I am always here, right here,
Even if you feel, I am far away,
I am not I am just here.

My arms are always open,
And as you encounter the storms of life,
Remember I am right here.

I love you, I will never leave you,
Or forsake you.
I am Your Father
I love you with an everlasting love.

Chapter 6
A Different Kind of Message

I felt the Lord want this book to be raw and real for those that travel through the valleys. I want to share a poem that I wrote in the early days of this journey.

A broken heart
I wish I could turn the clock back,
I wish you were still here,
I wish, I wish,
My hope is gone.

My eyes look to you Lord,
How do I go on?
How Lord?
I can't see it; I can't do it.

I am struggling with my loss,
My grief,
One step at a time.
One thing at a time.

Lord, hold my hand and lead me on,
A mother's broken heart,
It's overwhelming,
It doesn't feel real,
What to think?
What to do?

Do you care? – Yes, you do.
It's just different feeling for me and you,
A bump that was there,

Which now has gone,

Your time will come,
But for me at this moment,
It's come and gone.

The pieces,
I try to fit together,
To see myself as I once was,
But I see her tears, her heart,
I see the weakness,
The tiredness in her eyes,
The numbness, as she tries not to cry,
The aching in her heart for the baby that is lost.

But chin up not all is lost,
The days will get easier, the pain will ease,
But the mother's loss shall decrease,
The aching in her heart,
Will eventually subside.

But at the moment,
Take one day at a time.

It makes me cry just reading it, but this is a real story. A real life, the struggle, the pain and the dark days but I also want to encourage you. After the storm, comes a rainbow, the days will and do get easier, take one step at a time. Minute by minute, hour by hour, day by day. One step at a time. Be kind to yourself and let you self-grieve. Everybody is different and people are different, it may not affect someone as much as you. The healing process may take more time for you, you can't put a time limit on grief.

God the helper of those who seek Him. Psalm 121 v 1–2

I lift my eyes unto the hills,
From whence cometh my help.
My help comes from the Lord,
Who made the heavens and the earth.

A letter to me.

What your about to go through is going to floor you, in ways you never thought possible or even understood.

So here are a few suggestions to get you through.

Look after yourself and be kind. Sometimes we are too busy looking after others, so make time for yourself.

Have a nice walk, go out for the day, do things you enjoy. Make time to read a book. Pamper yourself, watch a good film.

Your body will tell you what you need, listen to it. Rest, sleep, cry, go through the emotions, don't fight them. This can cause other problems later on down the line, like depression and physical symptoms.

Every step is a goal, if that's just getting out of bed in the morning. If that's making breakfast. Having a shower. The little things we take for granted. Do things you enjoy, take time out for you. Praise yourself for the little thing you do. Small steps make a massive difference, start small. Remember one minute at a time, one hour at a time, one day at a time.

Ride the rollercoaster of emotions, be sad, cry, laugh, shout, scream, into a pillow if needed. Go to a field if you need to, get a teddy and throw it around the room, go bowling. Find ways to deal with your emotions appropriately. Exercise, run, join a gym. Being physical with someone else is not appropriate. Get counselling if you need to. The miscarriage association have been a great support to me, we also had regular visits with our pastor at church. I can't tell you how much this helped and supported us. Spend time with a friend, go for coffee. Do a little shopping. Be careful you don't form bad habits.

Take a deep breath, just breath in and out. Sit in the garden, go for a walk. One step at a time, One day at a time. Go and see a friend, spend time with people you love.

Don't try to run before you can walk. Keep a journal, write things down, do something creative. Use different avenues to manage your emotions. Drinking and drug taking is not the answer.

Give your self-time. People will say the wrong things at times, they are only trying to help. Its ok to draw back from friends and family that have children or are pregnant. Even from the world, just for a time to re-group and re-gather. Things, situations can be too painful at the moment, too many memories. That ok just takes time. Be kind to yourself.

Don't put yourself in situation that will be too painful. Its ok to withdraw until you are ready to face it again. You will, just not yet. Be kind to yourself. This may be very hard to do but you need to find time. Even if its ten minutes a day.

I want to share one last thing with you.

April 3rd 2021

I just need to look and see how far I have come. This book (my writing Journal) is a sign of how far we have come and the days, I have overcome.

Some of these days have been the hardest, I have ever had to face but I did. It is now two years on and I still get upset and emotional. Little thing will sometimes set me off. Like seeing a little girl with her daddy, a baby in a pram, a song, a baby outfit. I have overcome by taking one step at a time, one day at a time, listening to my body, support from my loving husband, family and friends and our church.

I am very blessed, now I can reach others that are going through the same and be a support and encouragement to them through this book. It has not been easy for me to write this book, I have re lived days and emotions, but I also believe this is another part of my healing process. This is a process, step by step, day by day. Grief is a process and we do, go through the different stages and emotions. Grief can be any kind of loss, a person, a pet, a relationship, friendship. This was grief on a larger scale for me. I have lost family member very close and not so close, close friends but this hit me harder than any of them. This stopped me in my tracks, knocked me down, I could not function. With help from our church, family, friend and miscarriage association, I have learned to look after myself and be kind, talk and express my feeling and emotions in the right way. Not to fight my feeling and emotions and not to suppress them. Just to take each day as it comes, if I am having a bad day, minute by minute, hour by hour. Tomorrow is a new day. New page to start again. Little steps, go with the emotions don't fight them.

The Lord gave me this scripture and the reason for writing this book.

2 Corinthians 1 v 3–4
Blessed be the God and Father of our Lord Jesus Christ, the Father of mercies and God of ALL comfort, who comforts us in ALL our tribulations, that we may be able to comfort those who are in any trouble, with the comfort with which we ourselves are comforted by God.

Father God,

I pray that those who are reading this book and are going through their own trials and storms. And who have been touched by my story, I pray Father, You cover them and protect them just as You did with me. I pray You surround them with Your love and peace. And that they know that this storm will pass by, and You are right there with them. Comfort them Father just as you did, with me. Amen

Psalm 91 v 1–2
He who dwells in the secret place of the Most High Shall abide under the shadow the shadow of the Almighty.

Also by Michelle Mapplebeck

ISBN: 978-1-910779-62-0

Buy from Amazon

Ingram Content Group UK Ltd.
Milton Keynes UK
UKHW050645200623
423735UK00007B/36